FOSTER
CLASSROOM QUESTIONS WITH COMPARATIVE STUDY

A SCENE BY SCENE TEACHING GUIDE

Amy Farrell

SCENE BY SCENE
ENNISKERRY, IRELAND

Copyright © 2017 Scene by Scene

Without limiting the rights under copyright, this book is sold subject to the condition that it shall not, by way of trade or otherwise be lent, resold, hired out, reproduced, stored on or introduced into a retrieval system, or transmitted, in any form or by any means (electronic, mechanical, photocopying, recording or otherwise), or otherwise circulated, without the publisher's prior consent, in any form other than that in which it is published and without a similar condition, including this condition, being imposed on the subsequent publisher.

All rights reserved. No part of this publication may be recorded or transmitted in any form or by any means electronic, mechanical, photocopying, recording or otherwise without the proper consent of the publisher.

The publisher reserves the right to change, without notice, at any time, the specification of this product, whether by change of materials, colours, format, text revision or any other characteristic.

Scene by Scene
Enniskerry
Wicklow, Ireland.
www.scenebysceneguides.com

Foster Classroom Questions/Amy Farrell. 2nd ed.
ISBN 978-1-909417-70-2

Contents

Chapter One	1
Chapter Two	9
Chapter Three	14
Chapter Four	18
Chapter Five	20
Chapter Six	33
Chapter Seven	36
Chapter Eight	40
Further Questions	47
Theme/Issue (HL)/Relationships (OL)	50
Cultural Context (HL)/Social Setting (OL)	56
Literary Genre (HL)	61
General Vision and Viewpoint (HL)	68
Hero, Heroine, Villain (OL)	75
The Comparative Study: Comparing Texts	78

Chapter One

Summary

Early on a Sunday morning, instead of taking her home, the girl's father drives into county Wexford after mass.

She considers what the Kinsellas' place will be like, imagining different versions of it.

When they arrive, the man who comes out to them looks nothing like her mother's people, and she wonders if they have come to the wrong house.

The men talk about the lack of rain and farming.

The woman comes out, takes the girl out of the car and kisses her. The woman has not seen her since she was a baby.

She wipes the girl's face. The girl knows how dishevelled she must look in the woman's eyes.

The woman leads the girl into her clean kitchen and asks after the girl's mammy.

The girl remembers her mother fixing her hair that morning, asking her father how long the Kinsellas should keep her for. He replied that they could keep her as long as they liked.

The girl tells the woman they have not cut their hay yet.

The men come in. The woman's voice changes when she speaks to Dan, the girl's father.

He talks about how much hay they have taken in and the girl wonders why he is lying.

The girl wishes she was out working. She wants to go home with her father, but also wants to stay here.

Kinsella sets out food for their meal.

The woman asks after Mary and Dan says she is nearing her time (her due date). He remarks that children have big appetites and tells the Kinsellas that they can work the girl. Kinsella says there will be no need for that.

Once he has eaten, her father is keen to be on his way.

With the girl's mother, it is all work. She realises this is a different type of house.

Her father says he has to go and spray potatoes.

The woman goes and cuts rhubarb for Mary. The girl's father drops some and waits for the woman to pick it up, but she does not.

He gets into the car. Before leaving, he tells the girl to try not to fall in the fire.

The girl wonders why he left without saying goodbye or telling her when he would be back for her.

The Kinsellas ask her what is wrong. The woman suggests it is because her father forgot all about her 'bits and bobs'. Kinsella says they will have her togged out in no time.

They laugh at something her father said.

The woman tells her it is time for a bath.

Questions

1. Where does this story begin?

2. What are the girl and her father doing?

3. Why does the girl mention Shillelagh? What does this tell you about her father?

4. How do they pass the time on their journey?

5. How does the speaker imagine life with the Kinsellas?

6. Describe the Kinsellas' house.

7. What makes the girl think they have arrived at the wrong house?

8. Who is John Kinsella?

9. What does the conversation between the men tell you about their background and lifestyle?

10. Describe the woman, Mrs. Kinsella (Edna).

11. How does the girl respond to being kissed by the woman? Can you explain her reaction?

12. How does the girl picture herself when she sees herself through the woman's eyes?

13. Is the girl very perceptive?
    Give a reason for your answer.

14. Describe the Kinsella's kitchen.
    What does it reveal to you about the Kinsellas?

15. The girl says, "There is no sign, anywhere, of a child."
    Why, do you think, is this significant?

16. What did the girl's mother spend her tenner winnings on?
    What does this tell you about her?

17. 'Can't they keep her as long as they like?'
    What is happening here?
    What is your response to the girl's father's words?
    How does this make you feel?

18. Does the woman like Dan, the girl's father, do you think?
    Refer to the text to support your answer.

19. What does the girl's father say about the hay this year?
    What is her response to this?
    What is your response to it?

20. Why does the girl wish she was outside, working?
    What insight does this give you into her life?

21. Is the speaker happy to be staying with the Kinsellas, in your opinion?
    Give a reason for your answer.

22. What does Kinsella set out for their meal?

23. Describe the conversation as they prepare to eat.
    What is the atmosphere like?

24. 'She'll ate but you can work her.'
    What does Dan's comment mean?
    How does this line make you feel?

25. How does Kinsella respond to this comment?
    What does this tell you about him?

26. What makes the girl's father keen to leave?

27. How does the girl describe things with her mother?
    What picture are you forming of their life?

28. In what ways is this house different to her own?
    Why, do you think, has the girl realised this already?

29. What excuse does her father make to leave?
    Do you believe him here? Why/why not?

30. The rhubarb is "awkward as the baby in my father's arms."
    What does this tell you about the girl's father and home?

31. What happens when the speaker's father drops some rhubarb as he prepares to leave?
    Is there anything significant in this gesture, in your opinion?

32. What does her father say to her as he leaves?
    What is your response to his words here?
    How would you feel, if you were the girl?

33. How does the girl feel, watching her father drive away?
    Do the Kinsellas know how she is feeling?
    Give a reason for your answer.

34. What are your first impressions of the speaker, her father, and the Kinsellas, in this opening chapter?

35. Has the girl been given away?
    Give reasons for your answer.

36. How would you feel if you were in the girl's position?

37. Does the girl seem upset to be away from home?
    Does this tell you anything about her home or family?

38. The first thing they will do, once her father leaves, is give her a bath.
    What does this tell you?

39. Why, do you think, have these people taken the girl in?

40. What is the Kinsellas' house like?
    Does this tell you anything about the Kinsellas themselves?

41. Describe Mr. Kinsella (John).

42. Describe the speaker's father (Dan).

43. Describe the setting in the opening chapter.

44. What is life like for the speaker's mother, from what you have read in this chapter?

45.   What interests you in the story so far?

Chapter Two

Summary

The woman fills the bath for the girl. It is too hot, and deeper than any bath she has had before. The woman washes and scrubs her clean.

The woman finds some old clothes for her to wear in a chest of drawers.

The girl tells the woman that her mammy says they can keep her for as long as they like. The woman laughs and brushes her hair while the girl looks out the window.

The woman asks the girl if she would like to go to the well. The girl asks if it is a secret. The woman faces her and says there are no secrets in this house, as where there is a secret, there is shame.

The girl stops herself from crying. The woman puts her arm around her and says she is too young to understand, and the girl wishes she was at home.

The woman fetches the zinc bucket and they walk through the fields to the well.

The girl sees how different her reflection looks now that she is clean, in different clothes. She drinks the well water and wishes this was her home.

The woman fills the bucket and they walk home hand in hand, the girl certain that she is balancing the woman.

The girl does not have to kneel and pray at bedtime. The woman does not hang a blanket on the curtain rail when she realises the girl is afraid of the dark.

The woman asks if her mammy is alright and whether she would be offended if the woman sent her some money.

She kisses the girl goodnight.

The wallpaper in the girl's room is covered in trains. She thinks of home.

Later, the woman comes in and sits on her bed. She says if the girl were hers, she would never leave her in a house with strangers.

Questions

1. The girl is glad that the Kinsellas sleep together.
   Why, do you think, might she feel this way?

2. What does the girl's bath reveal to you about her home life?

3. What does the woman dress her in?
   Does the girl mind wearing these clothes?
   What does this tell you about her?
   Would you mind? Give a reason for your answer.

4. The girl's father dropped her here with no clothes of her own.
   What does this tell you about her father?
   What does this tell you about the girl's life?

5. 'She says you can keep me for as long as you like.'
   How does this line make you feel?
   What does it tell you about the girl's home life?

6. What does the girl see out the window?
   What do you notice about this imagery?

7. How does Mrs. Kinsella react when the girl asks if going to the well is a secret?
   What does this tell you about the woman?

8. How does the woman correct the girl's speech?
   Why does she do this, do you think?
   How would you feel about this, if you were the girl?

9. Why does the girl wish she was at home?
   Describe how she is feeling here.

10. How do they get to the well?

11. Describe the well.

12. What does the well water taste of?

13. What does the girl wish, as she drinks the water?
    Does this surprise you? Why/why not?

14. How does she feel as they walk home together?
    How does this make you feel?

15. What questions does the woman ask her at bedtime?
    Why does she ask these questions?
    What do the girl's answers reveal to you?

16. Describe the wallpaper in the girl's bedroom.

17. What does the girl think about?

18. Why, do you think, does the girl pretend to be asleep when the woman comes in later on?

19. What does the woman say?
    How does this make you feel?

20. How old is the girl, do you think?
    Explain your estimate.

21. Is the girl lucky or unlucky to be staying here, do you think? Give a reason for your answer.

22. How does the woman feel towards the girl's parents, do you think?
    Why, do you think, has she taken this girl in?

23. Why does the woman want to send money to the girl's mother?
    What does this tell you about the woman?

24. Describe Kinsella's farm.

25. Is the girl confused about staying with the Kinsellas? Explain your point of view.

26. What does the last paragraph of this chapter tell you about Edna Kinsella, and also, the girl's family?

27. Is the mood happy or sad as this chapter ends? Explain your point of view.

Chapter Three

Summary

Mrs. Kinsella discovers that the girl has wet the bed. The girl wants to admit to it and be sent home.

The woman says that old mattresses weep. She does not say anything about the girl wetting the bed.

They bring the mattress outside and wash it, then the woman fixes rashers and tomatoes for breakfast. The girl helps.

When Kinsella comes in, he mentions that another hunger striker died in the night. This news makes him feel grateful for what he has.

The girl helps the woman around the house. The Kinsellas do not rush, but are always busy.

Later, Kinsella asks the girl to run to the postbox as fast as she can, to fetch the letters for him.

That night the woman says she is eating plain Weetabix for her complexion. The girl eats five of them as she watches the nine o'clock news, sitting in the woman's lap.

Before bed, the woman cleans the wax from the girl's ears, something her mother rarely has time to do, and brushes her hair.

The next morning, the girl has not wet the bed.

The woman tells her that all she needs, is minding.

Questions

1. How does Mrs. Kinsella react to the wet mattress?
   What does this tell you about her personality?

2. Are you surprised that the girl wet the bed?
   What stopped her from telling the woman about it, do you think?

3. How does the girl help the woman prepare breakfast?
   Are they getting on well together?

4. Kinsella mentions that he heard on the news that another hunger striker died.
   What does this refer to?
   What time period does this place the story in?

5. Why does Kinsella feel grateful?

6. How does the girl spend her day?

7. Are the Kinsellas busy people?

8. What job does Kinsella give the girl?

9. What is the woman doing to work on her complexion?
   Is this really the case?
   What is going on here?

10. What news items are on the nine o'clock news?
    Does this tell you anything about the world of the novel?

11. Where does the girl sit during the news?
    What is your response to this?

12. Why doesn't the girl's mother clean her ears?
    What picture are you forming of the girl's home?

13. What is different the next morning?

14. How is the woman feeling?
    What makes her feel this way?

15. As this chapter ends, the woman tells the girl that all she needs is minding.
    Is this true, do you think?
    How do the woman's words make you feel?

16. Are the Kinsellas treating the girl well, in your view?
    Give reasons for your answer.

17. What is the mood like, as the chapter ends?

18. Based on what you have read so far, describe the girl, as you imagine her to be.

19. Do you expect the girl to be happy here?
    Why/why not?

Chapter Four

Summary

The days pass. The girl waits to make some mistake, but it does not happen.

They spend their days together, doing jobs around the house and garden.

Sometimes, people come and play cards with the Kinsellas at night. One time the woman brings the girl down with them. The Ass Casey makes so much noise when he laughs, she would not get any sleep anyway.

Questions

1. What is the girl waiting for as the chapter begins? Does this tell you anything about her or her life?

2. How does the speaker spend her time with the Kinsellas? Is she happy here, do you think?

3. Does she have to work very hard for the Kinsellas?

4. Are the Kinsellas part of their community? Explain.

5. Do the Kinsellas sound sociable? Explain.

6. How do the Kinsellas spend their time when people visit at night?

7. How did the Ass Casey get his name?

8. Is this a happy household, in your view? Give reasons for your answer.

9. Do the Kinsellas care about the girl, do you think?

10. Is the speaker happy in her new home? Explain your answer.

Chapter Five

Summary

They are preparing gooseberries for jam one afternoon when Kinsella comes in and tells the girl it is time they got her new clothes.

The woman objects, saying she is clean and tidy, but Kinsella wants her to have new clothes for Mass the next day.

The woman finishes the gooseberries, sighs and goes to get ready.

Kinsella is troubled by something. He speaks sharply to the girl, telling her to wash her hands and face before they go to town, asking if her father did not teach her that much.

The girl rushes to the bathroom, but the woman is in there, crying. She says it will be nice for the girl to have her own clothes.

Town is crowded and busy. Kinsella gives the girl a pound and tells her to get a Choc-ice. She stares at the note. He says she is for spoiling.

The woman takes her to the draper's where the girl tries on new clothes. The assistant assumes they are mother and daughter, and Edna does not correct her.

The woman buys new clothes and shoes for the girl.

They meet people the woman knows who ask who the girl is. One woman remarks that she is good company for her and Mrs. Kinsella makes an excuse and leaves.

They go to the butchers, chemists and gift gallery, where they buy a card for the girl's mother. The woman says her birthday is coming up, although the girl is unsure.

The shopkeeper says it will be great when the children go back to school. The woman replies that the girl is no trouble, and that she will miss her when she is gone.

They visit a sweet shop before going back to the car. They eat sweets on the way home.

There is a woman waiting in their yard. Michael has died and she cannot get word to her family as they are all out on the combines. She asks John to help her dig a grave.

The woman cannot leave her behind, so the girl gets changed and they start walking to the wake. There is a sense of something dark in the air, a change that is about to occur. The animals they pass are jumpy and the wind blows hard and soft.

The woman asks the girl if she has been to a wake before. She lets her know there will be a dead man in a coffin, and people drinking.

The house is packed with people, and at their centre lies the dead man in his coffin.

Kinsella sits her on his lap and gives her a taste of his drink. The girl drinks red lemonade and eats biscuits, looking at the dead man.

The girl gets bored. Mildred, a neighbour, offers to walk the girl home. Mrs. Kinsella agrees, saying they won't be long.

Once they round the bend, Mildred starts asking questions about the Kinsellas and their home.

The girl answers them easily until Mildred asks if the child's clothes are still in the wardrobe.

When the girl mentions her outfit, Mildred says she is dressed as if she is going on for a hundred. She adds that it is better than wearing the dead's clothes, and calls her a dope for not knowing about the Kinsellas' son, who followed their dog to a slurry tank and drowned.

Mildred says John was too softhearted to shoot the dog afterwards.

She adds that the Kinsellas' hair turned white overnight, and laughs when the girl says Mrs. Kinsella's hair is black.

The girl wonders that she did not figure this out for herself.

They arrive at Mildred's. She sits down and talks about the details of the wake.

CLASSROOM QUESTIONS • 23

Kinsella arrives for the girl. He thanks Mildred for taking her home.

Out in the car, the woman asks if Mildred asked the girl questions. The girl tells them what Mildred asked her. She says that Mildred told her about their little boy drowning in the slurry tank, and her wearing his clothes to Mass last Sunday.

When they get home, the hound comes out to them. The girl realises the Kinsellas do not call it by name.

The woman gets ready for bed and Kinsella and the girl go for a walk.

Kinsella holds her hand, something she realises her father has never done. Part of her wants him to let go, so she will not have to feel this.

They walk down to the sea together. They climb a hill and look across the water towards England. Two bright lights blink out in the darkness.

The girl runs down the dune to the sea. She runs back and forth, shrieking as the waves crash in.

They take off their shoes and walk in the water together.

Kinsella talks of fishermen finding horses at sea. He says that sometimes strange things happen, as happened the girl tonight.

He says it was not Edna's fault, that she is too trusting, looking for the good in others.

He tells the girl that you do not ever have to say anything. He tells her to remember this.

The night feels strange to the girl, walking to the sea in the dark and listening to the man's words.

They walk as far as they can before turning back. The girl gathers shells.

A cloud covers the moon and Kinsella lights the lamp. They follow their tracks back the way they came. Kinsella puts their shoes back on.

Looking out to sea they see three lights where before there were two. Kinsella puts his arms around the girl and gathers her into them as though she were his.

Questions

1. What job are the girl and woman doing when Kinsella comes in?

2. What does Kinsella want to do?
   Why does he want to do this now?

3. Does the woman, Edna, agree with him?
   Give a reason for your answer.

4. Is there tension in the house before they go to Gorey?
   What details make you say this?
   Have you any idea what could be going on here?

5. How does the girl know that Kinsella is troubled by something?
   Is the description here effective?

6. How does Kinsella speak to the girl?
   How does she respond?
   Are you surprised to hear him speak to her like this?
   Is this a hurtful comment to make?
   Why does Kinsella say this?

7. Where is the woman?
   What is going on here, do you think?
   How would you be feeling, if you were the girl?

8. What is Gorey town like?

9. What does Kinsella give the girl?
   How does she respond?
   Can you explain her response?

10. How has the mood changed?

11. Where does the woman take her?

12. 'She's the spit and image of her mammy. I can see it now.'
    What does the shop assistant assume?
    Why doesn't the woman correct her?

13. What does Edna buy for the girl?

14. "We meet people the woman knows."
    How do the woman's acquaintances react to the girl?
    How would you feel, in her position?

15. What remark does the woman with eyes like picks make about Edna having the girl to stay?
    Does she sound kind or condescending to you?

16. Are you surprised that the girl is not sure when her mother's birthday is?
    Does this tell you anything about the girl's home?

17. 'It's only missing her I'll be when she is gone.'
    Is Mrs. Kinsella talking about school here?
    Do characters in this novel often make remarks with deeper meanings than they appear at first?

18. What does the girl spend her money on?
    Does she spend it all on herself?

19. Are the Kinsellas kind to the girl in Gorey? Explain.

20. Why is Harry Redmond's girl waiting for Kinsella (John) when they return?
    What does this tell you about the community they live in?

21. 'John's not always easy but he's hardly ever wrong.'
    From what we have read so far, do you think John and Edna Kinsella have a good relationship?
    Use examples to support your view.

22. What is the atmosphere like, as they walk down the road?

23. What do you notice about the behaviour of the animals they pass on their way to the wake?
    How does this add to the mood here?
    What other details help create the mood?

24. How does the author build tension on the way to the wake?

25. Describe the farmland they walk through.

26. Why, do you think, does Edna ask the girl if she has been to a wake before?

27. Describe the wake.
    What do people do at the wake?
    What do they talk about?

28. Does it sound like a typical wake to you?
    Give reasons for your answer.

29. What does the wake tell you about the customs and beliefs in this community?

30. Why does the girl go home with Mildred, the Kinsellas' neighbour?

31. What starts once they round the bend?
    What is your response to this?
    What do Mildred's questions tell you about her?

32. What does Mildred say about the girl's outfit?
    What is your reaction to this?

33. What does Mildred reveal to the girl?
    Comment on the way she tells her this news.
    What is your reaction to this?
    Why, do you think, does Mildred reveal this to her?

34. What happened to the Kinsellas' son?
    How would you feel at this moment, if you were the girl?

35. Knowing what you now know about the Kinsellas, were there any hints that their lives contained a tragedy like this? Explain your view.
    How does this piece of information change things?
    Does it make sense of anything for you?
    Explain, including examples from the text.

36. What comments does Mildred make about the Kinsellas?
    What kind of neighbour is she, in your view?
    Is she sympathetic towards the Kinsellas?
    Give a reason for your answer.

37. How does the speaker feel when Mildred reveals the story of the Kinsella boy to her?

38. The girl wonders how she did not realise about the Kinsellas' son sooner.
    Is she being hard on herself, or should she have figured this out for herself?

39. What is Mildred's house like?

40. What does Mildred talk about when she gets home?
    Does this surprise you?

41. Is Mildred surprised to see John so soon, do you think?

42. What does the woman ask the girl, out in the car?

43. What have the Kinsellas realised about Mildred?

44. When asked, how does the girl sum up what Mildred told her?
    What is your response to this?
    How would you feel if you were John or Edna?

45. What does the girl realise about the hound when they get home?
    Why is this significant?

46. What does John do to the girl's shoes before they go for a walk?
What does this detail tell you about him?

47. "As soon as he takes it, I realise my father has never once held my hand, and some part of me wants Kinsella to let me go so I won't have to feel this."
How does reading this make you feel?
Explain the girl's conflicting emotions here.
Is this a happy or sad moment, in your view?

48. Kinsella calls the girl "Petal".
Does this tell you anything about him, or how he treats the girl?

49. Describe the scene as Kinsella and the girl walk to the beach and along the shore.
What do you notice about the imagery?

50. How does the girl play on the beach?
Can you imagine this scene clearly?
What details in particular do you notice?
What is the mood like during the night visit to the sea?
Refer to the text to support your ideas.

51. What story does Kinsella tell about fishermen and horses?
Why does he tell this story?

52. "A strange thing happened to you tonight but Edna meant no harm…"
How does Kinsella explain Edna's trusting nature?
What insight does this give you into how he views and

feels about his wife?
What does this tell you about Kinsella himself?

53. What advice does Kinsella give the girl?
Is this good advice, do you think?

54. "Everything about the night feels strange…"
Comment on the atmosphere here.
How has the author created this atmosphere?

55. What makes Kinsella light the lamp?

56. 'Ah, the women are nearly always right, all the same,'
Does Kinsella have a positive view of women?
Is his view shared by the other men in the story? Explain.

57. What do they notice about the lights out to sea?
What is the significance of this?

58. Are they enjoying their time at the beach?
Give a reason for your answer.

59. Re-read the last sentence of this chapter again.
How does it make you feel?
Is this a touching scene?
Does Kinsella care about the girl, or does he miss his son?
How would you feel, if you were the girl?
How does this moment add to the story?

60. How do you feel about the way Mildred speaks to the girl in this chapter?
Why does she treat her like this?

61. In Chapter Two, Edna said, 'where there's a secret, there's shame.'
Do you think the Kinsella are ashamed of something?
Why did they keep this secret from the girl?
Were the Kinsellas wrong to keep this secret about the death of their son?

62. Does knowing about the death of their son change anything about how you feel about the Kinsellas?
Are they coping well with their loss?

63. What details from the story take on greater significance now that you know of the Kinsellas' loss?

Chapter Six

Summary

A letter arrives from home.

The girl has already noticed the signs in town of shops getting ready for the return to school.

The girl realises she is following Kinsella around, but cannot help it.

After the cows are milked, Kinsella sends the girl racing for the post. She is faster now than when she first came here.

Kinsella does not make jokes about the letters, but pauses when he sees one from her mother.

Edna reads it. The girl has a new baby brother. School is starting on Monday, so she is to go home at the weekend.

The girl asks if she must go home. Edna says she must, that she already knew she could not stay there forever.

The girl stares at the fire, trying not to cry.

The woman asks her to choose a pattern for the jumper she will knit her.

Questions

1. "...the letter comes."
   What will this letter mean for the girl?
   How do you feel about this?

2. What is significant about the approach of the new school year?

3. "I am following him around today, I realise, but I cannot help it."
   Why is she following him around, do you think?

4. Why doesn't Kinsella make jokes about the letters today?

5. What news is in her mother's letter?

6. 'I have to go back then?'
   Would you want to go home, if you were the girl?
   Give a reason for your answer.

7. 'You couldn't stay here forever with us two old forgeries.'
   What does Edna mean here?

8. How does the girl react to the news that she must return home?
   How do you feel about her going home?

9. What is the mood like as this chapter ends?

Chapter Seven

Summary

Knowing that she must go home, the girl almost wants to go, to get it over with.

The time she came to stay with the Kinsellas seems long ago.

Kinsella hangs around all day, working, but finishing nothing.

When they feed the calves, the girl asks him to take her home that evening, and he agrees.

The woman gives her a brown leather bag and they pack her clothes and books.

She remembers Kinsella helping her to read.

The woman gives her soap, her facecloth and hairbrush. The girl remembers getting these things, and their time together.

A neighbour calls, looking for John's help pulling a calf.

The woman goes to finish off the milking parlour.

The girl waits, restlessly. She decides to fetch water from the well, the last thing she will do here.

She puts on the boy's jacket and walks down through the fields. The way is muddy now, and the water level much higher than when she arrived.

The girl lets the bucket fill. She reaches down for it and sees her reflection, reaching for her. She falls into the well.

Questions

1. Has the girl changed much since coming to stay with the Kinsellas?

2. Will Kinsella miss her, do you think?

3. What makes the girl almost want to go home?
   How is she feeling?

4. Why does Kinsella hang around all day, do you think?

5. How does Kinsella respond when the girl asks to go home that evening?
   Is his response realistic and true to life?

6. What is the mood like at this point?

7. What does the woman give the girl?

8. How did Kinsella help the girl's reading?
   What does this tell you about him?
   What does this tell you about his relationship with the girl?

9. What else does the woman give to the girl?
   Why does she give her these things?

10. What does the girl think about as they gather her things together?
    What is the mood like at this point in the story?

11. The girl says that while she was with the Kinsellas, "the sun, for most of the time, was shining."
    Is there any significance in this detail for the reader?
    Has she enjoyed her time with the Kinsellas? Explain.

12. Why does Kinsella leave with a neighbour?
    What insight does this give you into the Kinsellas' community?

13. Why does the girl decide to go to the well?

14. How has the path changed since she first encountered it?

15. Describe the scene at the well.

16. What happens to the girl at the well?
    Is it entirely clear what happens here?
    Why did the writer phrase it like this, do you think?
    What is your response to this incident?

17. Is this a dramatic moment in the story?
    Why/why not?

18. Do you want the girl to go home to her parents?
    Refer to the text to support your view.

Chapter Eight

Summary

The girl is taken home two days later, on Sunday.

When she came back from the well, soaked to the skin, the woman put her to bed and brought her hot drinks.

The woman is very concerned about what could have happened to the girl.

The girl lies in bed, reading, dozing and thinking.

On Sunday they pack her things and drive her home.

Her house feels damp and cold. She notices the lino floor is dirty.

Her mother says she has grown and raises her eyebrows when the girl replies, 'yes'.

They have bread, butter and jam.

Kinsella asks after the new baby, who is sleeping.

Her sisters come over and look at her new clothes. They seem different to the girl.

Her mother fetches the baby when he wakes. The girl is embarrassed when her mother breastfeeds him in front of Kinsella. Her mother gives her a long look.

Kinsella asks after the girl's father, but her mother does not know where he went out to.

They chat a bit and then Dan arrives home. He asks if the girl gave the Kinsellas any trouble.

When Mrs. Kinsella says he will want to get his supper, Dan replies that he had a liquid supper in Parkbridge.

The girl sneezes and is defensive when her mother asks if she has caught a cold.

Dan makes a remark about how you can't mind children, making Mrs. Kinsella uneasy.

Kinsella says it is time to go home.

Her father says the girl has come home with a right dose, while her mother says it is going around.

The Kinsellas go out to the car and the girl follows. Kinsella gives her mother jam and potatoes. Her mother thanks him for taking her. They say she is welcome, anytime.

As the car starts to move off, Mary, the girl's mother, asks what happened. The girl says, 'Nothing', knowing she does not have to say anything.

The girl hears the car brake and sets off running down the lane. She thinks of the summer and of now.

She runs to the only thing she cares about, into Kinsella's arms. He hugs her for a long time.

When she finally opens her eyes, she sees her father coming.

The woman sobs in the car.

The girl wants to tell the woman that she will never, ever tell, but she stays in Kinsella's arms, holding on.

'Daddy' she says, both calling and warning Kinsella.

Questions

1. When is the girl taken home?
   Explain the delay here.

2. How does the woman feel about the girl falling in the well?
   Can you explain her concern?

3. Does Kinsella have a similar reaction?

4. How does the girl pass the time in bed?
   Is she well cared for?

5. On the journey home, the girl mentions her father losing the red heifer in a card game.
   Are you surprised that she tells the Kinsellas about this?

6. How has the girl changed since her arrival to the Kinsellas?
   Include as much detail as you can in your answer.

7. What does the girl notice about her house when she gets home?

8. How does the girl's mother greet her?
   Does anything about this surprise you?

9. How does the girl's mother react to her saying 'yes'?
   Can you explain this reaction?

10. What do they have to eat?

11. What do you notice about the girl's home?

12. How do her sisters respond to seeing her again?
How does she view them after the time apart?
How does this make you feel?

13. What is the atmosphere like in the girl's house? Use examples to support the statements you make.

14. How does the girl react to her mother breastfeeding the baby?
Explain her reaction.
How does this make her mother feel, do you think?

15. "…giving me another deep look."
Does the girl's mother know her well?

16. Where is the girl's father?

17. When Dan arrives, he calls the girl the prodigal child.
What does this reference mean?

18. Dan asks the Kinsellas if the girl gave them any trouble.
What does this tell you about how he views his daughter?

19. What has Dan had for supper?
What does this tell you about him?

20. How does the girl respond when her mother asks if she has a cold?
What makes her respond this way?

CLASSROOM QUESTIONS • 45

21. What remark does Dan make about minding children?
    Why, do you think, does he say this?

22. Why does Mrs. Kinsella look uneasy?
    What is going on here?

23. What different reactions do her parents have to the girl sneezing?
    Can you explain their responses?

24. What does Kinsella give Mary, the girl's mother, before leaving?

25. 'She's a credit to you, Mary'
    What does this mean?

26. Is it emotional when the Kinsellas say goodbye to the speaker at her house?

27. The moment the Kinsellas get into their car, the girl's mother asks what happened.
    Are you surprised by her question?
    Why doesn't the girl tell her mother about falling into the well?

28. What makes the girl run after the Kinsellas?

29. Comment on the language and imagery as the girl runs towards the Kinsellas' car.

30. "There is only one thing I care about now, and my feet are carrying me there."
    How does this line make you feel?

31. "For a long stretch, he holds me tight."
    Is this an emotional moment in the story?
    What different emotions are at play here?

32. What is the woman doing?
    Why is she doing this?

33. What makes the girl want to go to the woman?
    What stops her?

34. How well are the Kinsellas coping with returning the girl to her home?

35. Explain the last line of this story.
    What effect does this line have on you?

36. What makes the ending of this story sad?

37. Do you like the ending of this novel?
    Is there anything about it you would like to change?
    Why has the author, Claire Keegan, chosen to end it like this?
    What questions are you left with?

Further Questions

1. Who does the girl want to live with?
   Why can't she make this choice?
   What makes her situation so complicated?

2. Why is not telling about the well so important to the girl?

3. What problems do the girl's parents face?

4. What problems do the Kinsellas face?

5. Was sending the girl to live with the Kinsellas fair?
   Explain your answer fully.

6. The girl is always with the Kinsellas, helping them around the house and farm.
   Is her home like this, do you think?
   Give a reason for your answer.

7. Are the girl's family poor?
   Can you explain their financial situation?

8. What age is the girl, do you think?
   How has the girl changed by the time she comes home to her parents?
   What has brought about these changes in her?

9. After the story ends, will the girl be happy, do you think? What makes you say this?

10. Is loneliness a theme in this novel? Explain.

11. Why, do you think, is this story told from the girl's point of view? Explain.

12. Does this story teach us anything about people?
    Does it teach us anything about life?
    Refer to the text to support the points you make.

13. What is important to the characters in this text?
    How does this make you feel about them?

14. Do the characters in 'Foster' lead happy lives?
    Refer to the text to support your ideas.

15. How is family life portrayed in this novel?
    Is this a realistic picture of family relationships, do you think?
    Does this picture of family life still ring true today?
    Refer to the text to support your ideas.

16. Is the girl a good lead character?
    Give reasons for your answer.

17. Is the girl a likeable character?
    Give reasons for your answer.

18. Do you like how this story is told?
Consider the chapter structure, point of view, language and description, etc.

19. Who is your favourite character in the novel?
What do you like about them?

20. Who is your least favourite character in the novel?
What do you dislike about them?

21. What are the major themes and issues in this text?
How are they explored?
What conclusions do you draw?

22. What did you enjoy about this story?

23. What did you dislike about this story?

24. Is this novel engaging and thought provoking?
Explain your point of view.

25. Does this novel remind you of any novels you have read, or plays or films you have seen?
Explain your point of view, including examples to support your view.

Theme/Issue (HL)/Relationships (OL)

The theme of relationships can be applied to any relationship in a text and includes love, marriage, friendship and family bonds. Consider the complexities of relationships and the impact they have on characters' lives.

1. What does the section where her father drops her off to stay with the Kinsellas reveal about the girl's relationship with her father?
   How do you feel about the way her father treats her here?

2. Does the girl have a good relationship with her father? Include examples to support your view.

3. What do we learn of the girl's mother during the novel?
   Is she a good mother?
   Does she love her daughter?

4. Why has the girl been sent away?
   Does the girl know why she has been sent away?
   What does this suggest about her relationship with her parents?
   How does this make you feel?

5. Would you leave your daughter with relatives she had never met?
   Give a reason for your answer.

6. Does the girl love her parents?
What makes you say this?
Would you love them, if they were your parents?
Explain your point of view.

7. How does the girl's relationship with her parents change during her time with the Kinsellas?

8. Do the girl's parents have a good relationship?
Do they care about and support one another?

9. Does the girl have a good relationship with her mother?
Include examples to support your view.

10. Does the girl have a loving family?
Do her parents love her?

11. Do the girl's parents provide for her?
How does this affect their relationship with her?

12. What strengths do you see in the girl's relationships with her family?

13. What weaknesses or problems do you see in the girl's relationships with her family?

14. Are these positive or negative relationships?
Use examples to justify your view.

15. How do the Kinsellas treat her when she comes to stay with them?
Who benefits from this arrangement?

16. Does she miss her parents when she goes to stay with the Kinsellas?

17. How does the woman try to teach and help the girl?
How does the girl feel about this guidance?

18. Does the woman want to mother the girl, do you think?
Explain your point of view.

19. How do the Kinsellas feel about the girl?
How do they feel about her leaving?

20. Why don't the Kinsellas keep the girl?

21. Do the Kinsellas care about the girl, or are they trying to replace their son?
Support your point of view with reference to the text.

22. Why, do you think, did the Kinsellas take the girl in?
Do you think they were glad to do so, or regretted their decision?
Give a reason for your answer.

23. Are her aunt and uncle good foster parents?
Explain, giving examples.

24. Are the Kinsellas a positive or negative influence on the girl?

25. Do the Kinsellas love the girl?

26. How well do the girl and her parents communicate, interact and understand one another?

27. How well do the girl and the Kinsellas communicate, interact and understand one another?

28. How does learning of her cousin's death impact on the girl's relationship with the Kinsellas?

29. Do the girl's parents know her well?
Give examples in your answer.

30. Do the girl's aunt and uncle know her well?
Give examples in your answer.

31. Does the girl love her parents?
Does she love her foster parents?
Who does she love most, do you think?
Explain your view.

32. Does it matter who the girl loves most?
Is this difficult for the girl?

33. Who matters most to the girl?
Explain your choice.
How does this make you feel?

34. How do the girl's relationships with her parents change and develop during the novel?

35. How do the girl's relationships with her aunt and uncle change and develop during the novel?

36. How do the girl's family treat her when she returns home?
How does this make you feel?

37. Has the girl benefitted from her time with the Kinsellas?
    Has her time with the Kinsellas damaged her relationship with her parents?
    Explain your point of view.

38. How, do you think, do the Kinsellas and the girl's parents feel about each other?
    Include examples to support your ideas.

39. Do the Kinsellas have a good relationship?
    Do they care about and support one another?

40. Are relationships in this story positive or negative?
    Are they meaningful or shallow?
    What makes them this way?

41. What did you learn about relationships from reading this novel?

42. Are relationships portrayed realistically in this text?
    Make use of examples to support the points you make.

43. Are relationships in this story interesting and involving?
    Explain your point of view, using examples to illustrate your ideas.

44. What is the most significant relationship in this story?
    What makes this relationship stand out for you?
    What makes it so significant and important?
    What does it tell us about human relationships, friendship and love?

45. Are a lot of the relationships in this novel characterised by conflict?
Explain your point of view.

46. What else characterises relationships in this text? (Are they generally supportive, secretive, honest, loving, etc.?)

47. Do relationships in this story bring characters happiness or sorrow?
Include examples in your answer.

48. What makes relationships in this text complicated and difficult?

49. What helps relationships in this text?

50. What would improve relationships in this text?

51. How do relationships change during the story?

52. Does any aspect of the theme of relationships in this text shock, upset or unsettle you?
Use examples to help explain your point of view.

53. Choose key moments from this story that highlight relationships in the text.

Cultural Context (HL)/Social Setting (OL)

Cultural Context/Social Setting refers to the world of the text.
Consider social norms, beliefs, values and attitudes.

1. When the girl's father arrives at the Kinsellas, what do he and John talk about?
   What does this tell you about these men and their way of life?

2. When her father leaves, the first thing the woman does, is to bathe and clean the girl.
   What does this suggest about her home?
   What other details do you notice to support this view?

3. In Chapter Three, Kinsella mentions a hunger striker dying in the night.
   What does this reference tell you about this story's setting?

4. What chores fill the girl's days at the Kinsellas?
   What does this tell you about the place where she is living and the people she is living with?

5. Kinsella buys the girl new clothes for Mass on Sunday.
   What does this tell you about Mass?
   What does this tell you about this world?

6. A lot of money is spent in Gorey in Chapter Five.
   What does this tell you about the Kinsellas?

7. In Chapter Five, Harry Redmond's girl calls to the Kinsellas to ask John for help digging a grave.
   What does this detail tell you about this community?
   Is it similar to your own community in this way?

8. How does the wake in Chapter Five add to your understanding of this world and its customs?

9. How is the Kinsella boy's death in keeping with the novel's setting?

10. Is Mildred a good neighbour?
    What does she reveal about people in this community?

11. Are the Kinsellas part of a close-knit community?
    Give a reason for your answer.

12. Why was the girl sent to stay with the Kinsellas?
    Why can't they keep her?

13. What time and place is this story set in?

14. Describe the countryside where the story takes place.

15. How do the characters in this story make a living?

16. How do you know that the Kinsellas have more money than the girl's family?

17. What financial position is the girl's family in?
    How does her father spend his time and money?

18. What is life like for the girl's mother?

19. How does Kinsella spend his time and money?

20. What is life like for Edna Kinsella?

21. What attitudes are shown in the text through the character of Mildred, the neighbour who brings the girl home from the wake?

22. What are the Kinsellas' neighbours like?

23. Nobody ever discusses their problems or hardships in this novel.
    What does this tell you about the world of this text?

24. Does the girl have any say in the important decisions in her life?
    Why/why not?

25. Why can't the girl choose who she wants to live with?

26. Are her parents very different to her foster parents?
    In what ways are they different?
    What does this tell you about the world of the text?

27. Is this world a romantic or practical place?
Explain your point of view.

28. Are wealth and class important in this world?
What view do characters have towards money and class?

29. Is race important in this world?

30. Are characters in this text moral and upstanding?

31. What do characters value in this story?

32. What kind of society do you see in this text?
(How do people treat one another? What do they believe in? What is important to them?)

33. Is there violence and conflict in this world?
Where do you see this violence and conflict?

34. Is this a secure or dangerous world?

35. What is the role of women in the world of this novel?

36. How are women viewed and treated in this story?

37. How are children viewed and treated in this story?

38. Is family important in the world of this text?

39. What is the most important thing to characters in this world?
What is your response to this?

40. Are characters in this world free to live as they choose, or must they conform to society's expectations?

41. Is this world a supportive or destructive environment for the novel's characters?

42. Are friendship and love important in this world, or are characters self-centred and self-serving?
Justify your viewpoint with reference to the text.

43. Is their world a warm, loving place, or a cold, unfeeling place?
Justify your viewpoint with reference to the text.

44. Identify the key moments in the novel that illustrate the Cultural Context/Social Setting of the text.

45. Would you like to live in the world of *'Foster'*?
Include examples to justify your viewpoint.

46. How is the world of *'Foster'* similar to your world?
How is it different?
Use examples to support your point of view.

Literary Genre (HL)

Literary Genre refers to the way the story is told. Consider aspects of narration such as the manner and style of narration, characterisation, setting, tension, literary techniques, etc.

1. The girl has never been to the Kinsellas' place before the story begins.
   What does this add to the story for the reader?

2. The speaker is never called by name in this novel, she is always 'the girl'.
   Can you suggest a reason for the author leaving the girl without a name?
   What is the effect of this?

3. How does the author create a clearly defined sense of place in the opening chapter?

4. What effect(s) does Claire Keegan's nature imagery and descriptions of the natural world, have on the story?

5. Does the author give the reader hints and clues, or a direct, obvious plot-line in this novel?
   What makes you say this?
   How does this contribute to the storytelling?
   What is the effect of this on the reader?

6. How does the author create a sense of expectancy as the girl and the woman walk to the wake in Chapter Five?

7. How does the author make use of tension and reader anticipation in her narrative?

8. Mildred reveals the truth of the Kinsellas' dead son in Chapter Five.
How do you feel, reading Mildred's words here?
How does her revelation change your understanding of what went before?

9. Is the news of her cousin's death an unexpected twist?
What hints are there that something tragic happened in the Kinsellas' past?
What does this development add to the story?

10. How does the night walk to the beach add to the story?
Is this a moving or touching moment in the story?
Explain your point of view.

11. What do the three lights out at sea symbolise in Chapter Five?

12. How does Keegan use descriptions of the landscape to evoke mood and atmosphere in this novel?

13. How does the setting of the Irish countryside contribute to the story?

CLASSROOM QUESTIONS • 63

14. How does the author create the sense that a lot has changed during the girl's time with the Kinsellas?
What does this add to the story?

15. How does the author create the sense that the girl belongs in her new home?
What does this add to the story?

16. Is this a very emotional story?
Is this emotion often understated?
Does this increase or lessen its emotional power?

17. Is this a very visual text?
Use examples to support your viewpoint.

18. This novel is told exclusively from the girl's perspective.
What does this add to the story?
Why, do you think, did the author choose to tell her story this way?

19. Is the girl a good choice of narrator?
Explain your view.

20. The girl does not fully understand everything that is going on.
How does this add to the story?

21. How does the author create a sense of the girl's character?
Do you like this character? Why/why not?

22. How does the author create a sense of the girl's father?
Do you like this character? Why/why not?

23. How does the author create a sense of the girl's mother?
    Do you like this character? Why/why not?

24. How does the author create a sense of Kinsella (John)?
    Do you like this character? Why/why not?

25. How does the author create a sense of Mrs. Kinsella (Edna)?
    Do you like this character? Why/why not?

26. Is this novel about love, loss or something else?
    Give a reason to support the theme you identify.

27. How is this story told?
    Why is the story told this way?
    What is the effect of this?

28. What different aspects combine in the final chapter to make the ending moving and emotional?
    Refer to the text to support your point of view.

29. 'Foster' has been described as "beautiful, strange and moving."
    Do you agree with this assessment?

30. Identify the various sources of conflict in this text.
    How does the use of conflict add to the story?

31. Did you enjoy this story?
    Explain your answer, using examples from the text.

32. Does this novel have a satisfying ending?
Explain your point of view.

33. Comment on the mood as the story ends.

34. Consider the girl as the story's heroine.
What makes her an interesting or memorable character?

35. Do you find this novel to be interesting and easy to follow?
Include examples in your answer.

36. What three things interested you most in the story?

37. What draws the audience into this story?
Highlight specific aspects of the text in your answer.

38. Did you enjoy the storyline of the text?
Was it exciting, compelling, tense or emotional?
Use examples from the text to support your answer.

39. Is there just one plot or many plots?
What connections can you make between these storylines?

40. Who is your favourite character in this novel?
What makes you like/admire them?

41. Who is your least favourite character in this novel?
What makes you dislike them?

42. Do you empathise or identify with any characters?

43. Are characters vivid, realistic and well-developed?
Explain your point of view, using examples from the text.

44. What themes can you identify in this story?

45. Is this a sad tale?
Explain your point of view.

46. How does the author create suspense, high emotion and excitement in this text?
What techniques does she use to good advantage?

47. Consider the author's use of tension and resolution in the novel.
What are the major tensions/problems/conflicts in the text?
Are they resolved or not?

48. Does the author make use of any striking patterns of imagery or symbols to add to this story?

49. How does the author make use of the unexpected?
What does this add to the story?

50. What is the climax (high point) of the story?
What do you think of this moment?
How does it make you feel?

51. Comment on the language of the novel.
How does dialogue add to the story?

52. What do you find moving or emotional in this novel?

53. What aspects of the novel form worked well in this story, in your view?

54. What do you like about the way this story is told?

55. To what genre does this novel belong?
Support your choice with examples from the text.

General Vision and Viewpoint (HL)

General Vision and Viewpoint refers to the author's outlook or view of life and how this viewpoint is represented in the text.

1. How does the girl feel about staying with the Kinsellas in Chapter One?
   How would you feel, in her position?

2. What is the mood of the opening chapter?

3. The first thing the Kinsella woman does, once Dan leaves, is bathe and clean the girl.
   Explain her actions here.
   Does she care about the girl?

4. In Chapter Two, the girl tells the woman they can keep her as long as they like.
   How does this make you feel?
   What does this tell you about life?

5. Does the bed-wetting episode in Chapter Two demonstrate anything about the author's General Vision and Viewpoint?
   Explain your view fully.

6. The girl often mentions her family and home.
   What picture of this family are you forming?

Is it a positive or negative impression?
What sort of life do you think she has had?
What is your response to this?

7. How do you feel about the girl being sent to live with her aunt and uncle?

8. The girl is cared for and happy living with strangers.
How does this make you feel?
How do you feel about her return home?
What is Keegan telling us about life and how children are treated and valued?

9. The Kinsellas take the girl into their home and genuinely care for her.
What does this tell you about human nature?

10. What is the mood like on the trip to Gorey in Chapter Five?
What makes it this way?

11. In Gorey, the woman tells the woman in the gift gallery that she will miss the girl when she is gone.
Does their future parting hang over them?
Does the fact that their time together is fleeting taint it for them, or do they savour it?
Use examples from the text to support your point of view.

12. Do the Kinsellas want the girl, do you think?
Is this something happy or sad?
How do you feel for them?
How do you feel for the girl?

Why do they want her?
How does this make you feel?

13. Is life better or worse for the girl with the Kinsellas?
How do you feel about this?
What does this suggest about life?

14. What prompts Mildred to tell the girl about the Kinsellas' dead boy, in your opinion?
What does this reveal about human nature?
How does this development add to your understanding of the Kinsellas' lives?

15. Are the Kinsellas coping well with their loss and grief?
Are they resilient?
How does this detail contribute to the General Vision and Viewpoint of the novel?

16. Is the gaining of knowledge and loss of innocence, painful in this story?
What is the author suggesting about life?

17. "I think about the woman in the cottage, of how she walked and spoke, and conclude that there are huge differences between people." Chapter Five
What has the girl realised about people?
What do these differences involve?
Comment on how she acquired this knowledge.
How does this contribute to the novel's General Vision and Viewpoint?

18. What is the atmosphere like as Kinsella and the girl go walking by the shore at night?
How do you feel as you read this section?

19. At the end of Chapter Five, Kinsella hugs the girl as though she were his.
What does his love for this child tell you about people and life?
Is this a positive or negative aspect of human nature?
What does this suggest about the author's worldview?

20. What is going on beneath the surface of this story?
How does this affect the General Vision and Viewpoint of this story?

21. Does the girl want to live with the Kinsellas?
What lesson is the author demonstrating to us in this story?

22. Was it a kindness or cruelty to have the girl spend a summer with the Kinsellas?
Would she be better off never knowing their love?

23. Is the girl loved and wanted in this story?
Is this a positive or negative comment on life?

24. Did you want the girl to stay with the Kinsellas?
Explain your response.

25. How do you feel, reading about the girl's return home?

26. Is the girl's future promising?

27. Did you anticipate a happy ending to this story?

28. Does this story have a happy ending?
    What does it suggest about life?

29. How does reading the closing section make you feel?

30. Is there a lesson or moral to this story?
    What could it be?
    Does it still hold true today?

31. How do the adults in this story treat one another?
    What does this suggest about life?

32. Are the girl's parents happy with their lot in life?
    Are the Kinsellas happy and content?
    How does their happiness impact on the General Vision and Viewpoint of the text?

33. What is Claire Keegan telling us about life in this story?
    Is her message positive or negative in outlook?
    Explain your view

34. Are characters in this text hopeful and forward looking about life?
    Are they realistic? Do they make well-thought out plans?
    What does this suggest about their outlook on life?

35. What comments do characters make on their society and the problems they are facing?

36. Are characters happy or unhappy?

CLASSROOM QUESTIONS • 73

37. What makes characters in this story happy and fulfilled?

38. What makes characters in this story unhappy and unfulfilled?

39. Are relationships destructive or nurturing?
    What do they reveal about life as we see characters supported/thwarted in their efforts to grow/mature?

40. Is life full of possibility and potential in this text?

41. Are imagery and language bright or dark in the text? (Tone of the text)

42. What is the mood of this text?
    Include examples to justify your ideas.

43. Does this novel suggest that life is to be enjoyed or endured?
    Support your points with reference to the text.

44. What does this novel suggest about human nature?
    Is this outlook positive or negative?

45. Do characters face many obstacles and difficulties in this text? Do they struggle?
    Why/why not?

46. Is this text dark and bleak or uplifting and inspiring?
    Give reasons for your view.

47. What does this story teach us about life?

48. How do you feel as you read the novel?
    Refer to key moments to anchor your answer.

49. Does the novel end on a hopeful, optimistic note, or a hopeless, pessimistic one?
    Are questions raised by the text resolved by the end?
    Are they resolved happily or unhappily?
    How do you feel at the end?
    Explain your point of view.

50. Are you hopeful or despairing regarding the prospects for human happiness in this story?
    (Are characters likely to be happy?)

51. Identify the aspects of life that the author concentrates on.
    Are they positive or negative?
    What is she telling us by focusing on these aspects of life?

52. Identify bright, hopeful, optimistic aspects of the novel.

53. Identify dark, hopeless, pessimistic aspects of the novel.

54. Does this novel offer a comforting or disturbing view of life?
    Overall, is it optimistic or pessimistic?
    Explain your point of view.

Hero, Heroine, Villain (OL)

'Hero, Heroine, Villain' refers to central characters (protagonists/antagonists).

Their traits, values, etc. and their ability to deal with conflict, challenges, obstacles, etc. should be considered.

1. What are your first impressions of the girl?

2. What age is she, do you think?
   Include examples from the text to support your answer.

3. Choose three words that sum the girl up for you.
   Give reasons for your choices, referring to specific instances in the novel in your answer.

4. What was life like for the girl before she came to the Kinsellas?
   How has this affected her, as a person?

5. How does her life change during her time with the Kinsellas?
   How does this affect her?

6. How does the girl change and mature during her time with the Kinsellas?

7. What knowledge does the girl gain during her time with the Kinsellas?
   How does this knowledge change her?

8. Is the girl very obedient, do you think?
   Give a reason for your answer.

9. Is the girl a brave character?
   Explain your point of view.

10. Is the girl a happy character?
    Give reasons for your answer.

11. What problems does the girl face?
    Does she overcome these problems and difficulties?
    Why/why not?

12. At the start of the story, the woman tells the girl that she just needs minding.
    Is this true, do you think?
    Explain your point of view.

13. What confuses the girl in this story?
    What makes it difficult for her to solve the things that confuse her?

14. Is the girl better or worse off after her time with the Kinsellas?
    How does she feel about going home?

15. Do you feel sorry for the girl as the novel ends?
    Support your point of view with reference to the text.

16. What admirable qualities does the girl have?
    Explain your point of view, using examples from the text.

17. What strengths do you see in the girl's character?

18. What weaknesses do you see in the girl's character?

19. What does the girl value?

20. Does the girl cope well with change?
    What makes you say this?

21. How well does the girl cope with obstacles and challenges in her life?
    Use examples to support the points that you make.

22. Is the girl a happy and contented character?
    Explain your viewpoint fully.

23. What makes the girl an interesting character, in your opinion?

24. If you could chat to the girl, what would you talk about?
    What advice would you give her?
    What questions would you ask?

The Comparative Study: Comparing Texts

Use the following questions to compare your texts, noting the similarities and differences between them. Include examples to support the points that you make.

Theme/Issue - Relationships

1. Are relationships in this text more positive and supportive than the relationships in your other chosen texts?
   Include specific examples in your answer.

2. Rank the relationships you have studied in your various texts from most positive (score of 10) to most negative (score of 1).
   Add a note explaining your choices.

3. Are relationships in this text the most engaging and interesting that you have studied?
   Explain your choice.

4. Rank the relationships you have studied in your various texts from the most interesting (score of 10) to the least

interesting (score of 1).
Add a note explaining your choices.

5. How does conflict impact on the relationships of characters in this text and your other chosen texts?
Who is most affected?
Who is least affected?

6. How does social class impact on the relationships of characters in this text and your other chosen texts?
Who is most affected?
Who is least affected?

7. Is the theme of relationships portrayed in an idealistic or realistic way in each of your chosen texts?

8. Did any aspect of the theme of relationships shock or surprise you in your three chosen texts?
Use examples from your texts to support the points that you make.

9. What are the most interesting aspects of the theme of relationships in each of your chosen texts?

10. Which text taught you most about relationships?
Refer to each text in your answer.

11. Identify the key moments that best capture the theme of relationships in each of your texts.

12. What similarities do you notice in the theme of relationships in this text and your other Comparative Study texts?

13. What differences do you notice in the theme of relationships in this text and your other Comparative Study texts?

Literary Genre

1. Did you like the way this story was told more than your other Comparative texts?
State what you enjoyed most (and least) about each.

2. Is this text more exciting than your other texts?
Consider tension, suspense, pacing, conflict and the playwright's use of the unexpected.

3. How does the author make use of tension in each of your chosen texts?
Where is it most effective?
Where is it least effective?
Use examples to support your point of view.

4. How does the author make use of climax in each of your chosen texts?
Where is it most effective?

Where is it least effective?
Use examples to support your point of view.

5. How does the author make use of resolution in each of your chosen texts?
Where is it most effective?
Where is it least effective?
Use examples to support your point of view.

6. How does the author create vivid, memorable characters in each of your chosen texts?

7. In which of your texts are characters most life-like and compelling?
In which text are characters least life-like and most difficult to relate to?
Refer to each of your texts in your answer.

8. Are characters more engaging in this text than in your other texts?
Refer to each of your texts in your answer.

9. Is the setting more effective in telling the story in this text, than in your other texts?

10. Is setting more central to the story in this text or another text you have studied as part of your Comparative Study?

11. Is this text more unpredictable than your other texts?
Refer to each of your texts in your answer.

12. Does this text have greater emotional power than your other texts?
    Was this emotional power created in a more interesting way here or in a different text?
    Refer to each of your texts in your answer.

13. What was your favourite literary technique, used by the author of each of your texts?
    How did the use of this technique help the storytelling?

14. To what extent are you influenced by the point of view that this story is told from?
    Are you influenced to a greater or lesser degree by the point of view utilised in your other Comparative Study texts?

15. Identify the key moments that best capture Literary Genre in each of your texts.

16. What similarities do you notice in the Literary Genre of this text and your other Comparative Study texts?
    Mention specific aspects of narrative.

17. What differences do you notice in the Literary Genre of this text and your other Comparative Study texts?
    Mention specific aspects of narrative.

General Vision and Viewpoint

1. Is life happier and fuller for characters in this text than in your other Comparative Study texts?
   Explain your point of view fully.

2. Do characters in this text face more obstacles and difficulties than in your other texts?
   Who struggles most?

3. Are characters in this text rewarded more for their struggles than in your other texts?
   Do they overcome adversity and achieve true happiness and contentment in a way that is not realised in your other texts?

4. How do events in these texts, and your personal response to these events, help your understanding of the General Vision and Viewpoint of these texts?
   Include specific examples in your answer.

5. How does your attitude to central characters help shape your understanding of the General Vision and Viewpoint of your chosen texts?
   Include specific reference to your chosen characters in your answer.

6. Which aspects of this text did you respond to emotionally?
   How does this help your understanding of the General

Vision and Viewpoint of the text?
How does this compare to your other texts?

7. Is this the brightest, most hopeful and triumphant text you have studied?
Explain why its message is more or less positive than in your other texts.

8. Which of your chosen texts was the bleakest and most upsetting or depressing?
Explain what made it more negative than your other texts. What made them more positive?

9. Plot your three texts on a scale of one to ten from darkest (most pessimistic) to brightest (most optimistic). Add a note to explain their positions.

10. Identify the key moments that best capture the General Vision and Viewpoint of each of your texts.

11. What similarities do you notice in the General Vision and Viewpoint of this text and your other Comparative Study texts?

12. What differences do you notice in the General Vision and Viewpoint of this text and your other Comparative Study texts?

13. Can you relate any aspect of this text to your own life experience?
If so, how does this help to shape your understanding of the General Vision and Viewpoint of this text?

Cultural Context/Social Setting

Consider each of your chosen texts in your answers.

1. In which of the texts you have studied for the Comparative Study do characters have the most freedom and choice?
   Why is this the case?
   Justify your answer with examples from your chosen texts.

2. In which of your texts are characters most controlled?

3. Who holds the power in each world?
   Who is powerless?

4. In which world is difference most accepted and respected?
   In which world is difference least accepted and respected?

5. Which world is the least tolerant?
   Which world is the most tolerant?
   Include examples to explain your view.

6. Which world is the best to live in if you are a woman?
   Give reasons for your answer.

7. Which world is the best to live in if you are a man?
   Give reasons for your answer.

8. Which world is the best to live in if you are a child?
   Give reasons for your answer.

9. Which text portrays the most violent and volatile world?

10. Which of your texts portrays the safest, most secure place?

11. Which of your texts portrays the most supportive world?

12. Which of these worlds is the darkest, most fearful place?

13. Which of these worlds is the brightest, most joyful place?

14. Which of these places is the most unpredictable?

15. Which text portrays the most traditional world?

16. Which of these societies holds family in the highest esteem?

17. Which of these societies holds love in the highest esteem? Which of these societies holds love in the lowest esteem?

18. Which of these societies holds power in the highest esteem?

19. Which of these societies holds wealth in the highest esteem?

20. Where do you see the best treatment of the vulnerable of society? Include examples to support your view.

21. Where do you see the worst treatment of the vulnerable of society? Include examples to support your view.

22. Which of the worlds you have studied is the most materialistic?
Which of the worlds you have studied is the least materialistic?
What makes characters have these outlooks?

23. Which of the worlds you have studied is the most secretive?
What makes characters behave this way?

24. Which of your texts displays the greediest world?
What makes characters have this attitude?

25. Where is love most important?
Where is love most successful?
Where is love least important?
Where is love least succesful?
Compare the success of love in each of your chosen texts.
What does this tell you about the worlds of these texts and characters' lives?

26. Which of these worlds appealed to you most?
Give reasons for your answer.

27. Which of these worlds appealed to you least?
Explain your point of view.

28. Which of your texts is home to the most religious or spiritual world?
Which of your texts showed the least religious or spiritual society?

What effect does religion have on characters' lives in each of your texts?

29. How important is social class in each of your texts?

30. In which of your texts are characters most accepting of their world and society?

31. In which of your texts do characters challenge their world, society and values most?

32. In which of your texts do you see the greatest inequality?

33. In which of your texts do you see the greatest injustice?

34. Where do characters behave the best towards one another?
How does Cultural Context/Social Setting influence their behaviour?

35. How do characters reflect the Cultural Context/Social Setting of their worlds?
Explain, including examples.

36. How does the Cultural Context/Social Setting of your texts lead to problems and difficulties for the texts' characters?
How does it affect characters' responses to these difficulties?

37. Identify the key moments that best capture the Cultural Context/Social Setting of each of your texts.

38. What similarities do you notice in the Cultural Context/Social Setting of this text and your other Comparative Study texts?

39. What differences do you notice in the Cultural Context/Social Setting of this text and your other Comparative Study texts?

40. In which of your chosen texts did the Cultural Context/Social Setting most appeal to you?
Use examples to support your point of view.

Hero/Heroine/Villain

Consider the following list of questions for a central character in each of your chosen texts.

1. Who is the most interesting character in the text?
What makes them interesting?
What do you like about them?
What do you dislike about them?
What are this character's strengths?
What are this character's weaknesses?

2. How does this character cope with conflict?

3. How does this character cope with the unexpected?

4. Are they a resourceful character?

5. Are they an emotional character?
   Use examples to support your view.

6. Do you empathise with this character? Why/why not?

7. What do you admire about this character?

8. How well does this character relate to and interact with other characters?
   Include examples to support your points.

9. Is this character happy or sad?

10. Are they brave?
    Explain your point of view.

11. Are they an active or passive character?
    How do they contribute to the action and storyline of the text?
    Are they important to the story's plot and development?

12. Is this character a good (successful and interesting) main character?

13. Would you like to meet this character?
    If you met them, what would you talk about?

14. If you had any advice for this character, what would it be?

15. Does this character make the story more exciting?
    In what way do they do this?

16. Is this character a hero/heroine or a villain?
    Explain your choice.

17. Identify the key moments in the text that illustrate your chosen character's personality traits/character.

18. On a scale of one to ten (with one being extremely heroic and ten being an evil villain), where would you place your chosen character?
    Give reasons for your choice.
    Where would you place the main characters from your other texts?
    Why would you place them here?

19. Which of your chosen characters do you like and admire most?
    What makes them your favourite character?
    Give reasons for your answer.

20. Which of your chosen characters do you dislike most?
    Explain why you like some more than others.

21. Which of your chosen characters shocked you most?
    Give reasons for your answer.

22. Which of your chosen characters impressed you most?
    Give reasons for your answer.

23. Which of your chosen characters did you feel most sorry for?
    Give reasons for your answer.

24. Who is the most resourceful character you have come across?
    Give reasons for your answer.

25. Which of your chosen characters faced the most problems and difficulties?
    Did they cope well with these problems?

26. Choose key moments from each of your texts to highlight your characters' strengths and weaknesses.
    (One character per text).

27. How is your favourite character similar to the characters in your other texts?

28. How is your favourite character different to the characters in your other texts?

www.ingramcontent.com/pod-product-compliance
Lightning Source LLC
Chambersburg PA
CBHW071022080526
44587CB00015B/2461